D1434375

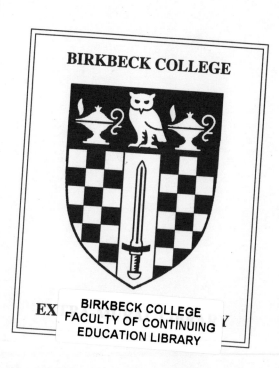

time machine

Ancient Egypt and Contemporary Art

Trustees of The British Museum

and

Institute of International Visual Arts

1994

…when I first visited the British Museum's Egyptian sculpture gallery, and saw the 'great arm' and imagined what the whole figure was like, which it had only been part of – then I realised how monumental, how enormous, how impressive a single piece of sculpture could be. Though it wasn't just the size alone which impressed me. Size and monumentality are not always the same thing. What I found in the Egyptian pieces was a monumentality of vision. henry moore

For the ancient Egyptians, art was creative in a fundamental sense, since it was regarded as actually 'bringing to life' for eternity whatever it represented. Imbued with a grandeur, a spirituality and a timelessness, their images have been copied, interpreted and reworked since antiquity itself, serving as a source of inspiration and of ideas for artists up to the present day. It is well known that the young Henry Moore was deeply influenced by what he saw in the British Museum's collections: 'In my most formative years, nine-tenths of my understanding and learning about sculpture came from the British Museum'. Egyptian sculpture, in particular, appealed to him for its 'monumentality of vision' and for what he regarded as its quality of stillness, 'a stillness of waiting, not of death'. Generously acknowledging this debt, Moore gave a substantial donation towards the cost of renewing the Museum's Egyptian Sculpture Gallery, which was completed in 1981.

Appropriately, it is this gallery that now acts as the venue for the special exhibition, **time machine** : *Ancient Egypt and Contemporary Art*, which aims to demonstrate that the creative link between the past and the present, so well exemplified in some of Moore's sculptures, is as strong and vital as ever and that collections such as those of the British Museum continue to play an enormously important role in the process.

The exhibition contains a remarkable range of pieces, produced by twelve contemporary artists, of varied backgrounds, for all of whom the themes and forms of Egyptian art have been somehow influential or have found a resonance within their own work. It includes sculptures, paintings, photographs and installation-pieces. Almost all have been created specially for the show and are being displayed among the antiquities which have helped to bring them into being.

The idea for **time machine** was that of James Putnam of the Department of Egyptian Antiquities, who has been responsible for most of its planning and organisation, and for the preparation of this catalogue. The mounting of the exhibition has been a collaborative effort involving not only this Department but also other sections of the Museum, in particular staff of the Museum's Design Office, Photographic Service, Building and Security Services, and Conservation Department.

The British Museum is very grateful to the Institute of International Visual Arts for co-producing the catalogue and collaborating with the Museum on an extensive programme of associated educational activities; to Momart PLC, The Arts Council of England, The London Arts Board, Pioneer High Fidelity (GB) Ltd, and Roxie Walker for their generous support of the project.

We are delighted and honoured that the Egyptian Ambassador, HE Dr Mohamed I Shaker, agreed to open the exhibition.

The exhibition could not, of course, have taken place without the participation of the contemporary artists themselves. We are enormously grateful to them for accepting our invitation and for rising to the challenge. May the art of the present, like that of the ancient Egyptians, 'live for ever and eternity'.

W Vivian Davies
Keeper of Egyptian Antiquities
British Museum

The art and culture of ancient Egypt have captured the imagination of successive generations of artists and writers in Europe but their aesthetic and intellectual significance have frequently been overshadowed by the privileged status accorded to ancient Greece and Rome in the European hierarchy of cultures. And yet, over the past hundred years, some of the most influential European artists have been inspired by the ancient Egyptians' way of seeing.

From Fernand Leger to Henry Moore, from Jacob Epstein to Richard Hamilton, the artistic ideas and forms of ancient Egypt have had a profound effect on modern European art. **time machine** : *Ancient Egypt and Contemporary Art* bears witness to the continuing importance of ancient Egypt for artists today from a range of different cultures and cultural backgrounds.

The Institute of International Visual Arts is dedicated to promoting the work of contemporary artists from a plurality of cultures and to creating a space for dialogue between cultures, past and present. We are, therefore, delighted to have the opportunity to collaborate with the British Museum on this exciting project which, we hope, will be the first of many such collaborations in the future. We are grateful to Vivian Davies, Keeper of Egyptian Antiquities, for his unflinching commitment and support of the project and to James Putnam, Curator of **time machine**, without whose boundless energy and vision this exhibition would not have been realised.

Contemporary art, like the art of ancient cultures, is too often perceived to be far removed from our present realities and everyday life. The exhibition **time machine** eloquently challenges these perceptions, bringing together the seemingly disparate worlds of Europe and Africa, the past and present, the museum and art gallery.

Gilane Tawadros
Director
Institute of International Visual Arts

Sandwork Andy Goldsworthy, 1994, temporary installation in the Egyptian Sculpture Gallery, British Museum (see page 48)

facing Period view of the Egyptian Sculpture Gallery

When I first saw ancient Egyptian sculpture I was awe-struck by its sheer power and intensity. I had not encountered quite such force and dynamism in any western art during my previous History of Art studies. Like all great religious art it is charged with a feeling of the eternal and superhuman, and it is not necessary to be a believer or an intellectual to appreciate this sense of presence. To the ancient Egyptians, art was a magical means of harnessing the energy they observed in nature's great cycle of birth, death and rebirth. Their art reflected the essential balance and harmony of the living world around them which they sought to maintain through religious ritual. Statues were regarded as receptacles for this divine force and they were intended for sacred places, rarely for mortal eyes. I am excited by these deeper qualities of ancient Egyptian art and its creators' need to express some intangible force and energy.

The artists invited by the British Museum to participate in **time machine** *are those who, it was felt, could express these particular qualities of Egyptian art; who would not simply draw directly on Egyptian images but would explore the concept in a more thematic and evocative way. Thus it was hoped to create both a more interesting and varied exhibition and a more sincere and meaningful contemporary perspective. To juxtapose the new with the old for shock value or as a way of reflecting current avant-garde art trends is certainly not the exhibition's intention. The participating artists feel a great sense of responsibility, even honour, at sharing an exhibition space with art that has been around for up to 5,000 years and 'stood the test of time'. I find it fascinating that our ideas about time itself have their origins in ancient Egypt. It was here that the year was* first divided into 365 days, the day into 24 hours, and the earliest clocks were invented. *I hope that the contemporary art shown here makes valid statements both for the concept and the space and succeeds in creating a harmony and conversation with the antiquities rather than merely a contrast. In this way, it also opens avenues for viewing the antiquities in a fresh light and not just as the remains of a dead civilisation.*

The creative force of the ancient artist lives on in his work, to be drawn on through time by successive generations. The British Museum is a great storehouse of human achievement, as much a place of inspiration as preservation.

James Putnam
Curator of **time machine**
Department of Egyptian Antiquities

david hiscock

David Hiscock, born in Hampshire, England, 1956, lives in London. He uses the photographic medium to explore different visual perspectives. His current work involves the use of a periphery camera, which is conventionally used to circumnavigate its subject. The zinc plates used in his exhibit have been manufactured with generous assistance from Studio Tone Ltd.

The main piece I have made for this exhibition is derived directly from the Rosetta Stone and has in its making formed a contemporary hieroglyph, a Bar Code.

A bar code symbol has no direct meaning, unlike the true hieroglyph, which can be a pictogram or a symbol for something. A bar code is merely a symbol which stands for a number; a binary code which merely states one or nought.

I am aware of time, Photographic time, Archaeological time, from a fraction of a second to many thousands of years. Connections to the past have left traces or resonances on film.

To hold in my hands ancient and sacred artefacts has been a unique and humbling experience. The connection between our world today and the ancient Egyptian seems too vast a gulf to contemplate. The Rosetta Stone bridges this divide. dh 1994

1

The Rosetta Stone takes its name from the town of Rosetta in the Nile Delta, where it was discovered in 1799. It has been on display in the British Museum since 1802. The stone is famous for its bilingual text written in three scripts: hieroglyph, demotic (both Egyptian) and Greek. Since the Greek could be read, it eventually provided the key to the decipherment of the Egyptian sections (196 BC, BM EA 24, granite, height 1.14 m)

2

Fragment of a basalt water-clock (about 320 BC, BM EA 938, height 35 cm)

1

2

david hiscock

3

4

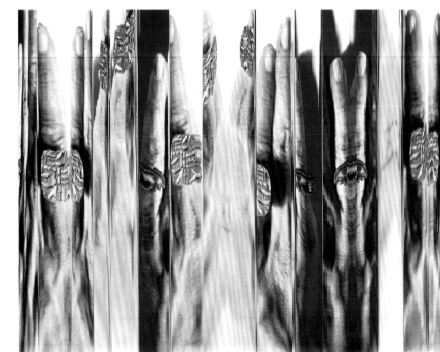

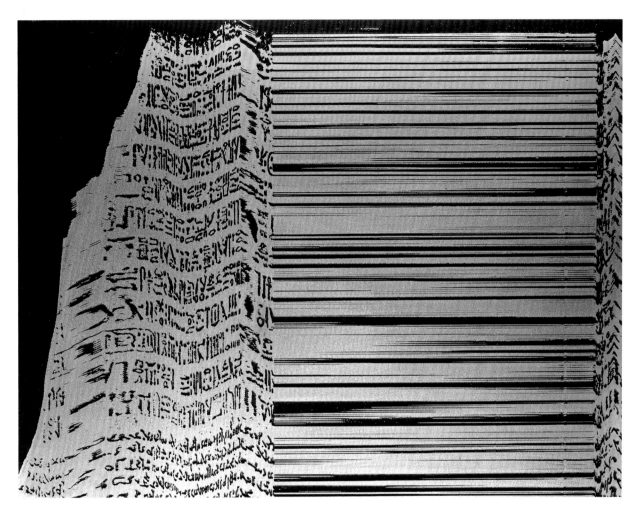

5

3
Water Clock David Hiscock, 1994, 5 × 4 transparency

4
Kiki Smith's hand wearing ancient rings David Hiscock, 1994,
5 × 4 transparency

5
Rosetta Stone bar code David Hiscock, 1994, etched zinc plate,
powder-coated and sand-blasted, 43.5 × 56 cm

time machine

rita keegan

Rita Keegan was born in New York in 1949 and has been living in
London since 1979. Her work involves a broad scope of media,
including computer generated images, a laser disk installation
and a real time surveillance monitor.

---

*Growing up in New York City is a mixed blessing, but the
Metropolitan Museum of Art definitely comes out on the plus
side. I was lucky to be introduced to it at an early age and I've
never looked back. The Museum and Radio City Music Hall were
my two favourite places and the 'Met' was number one.
Wandering through this treasure chest was always full of new
surprises. No matter how many times I visited and other things
that I discovered, or how my taste changed over the years, the
rooms in the Egyptian collection remained an essential visit.*

*It was only natural when I moved to London that I would
start to investigate and explore the British Museum. I had visited
the museum many times, when in the spring of 1989 I went to
sketch some of the goddess sculptures for a project I was working
on. I came across a statue of a seated couple who bore a striking
resemblance to my mother and father. It was the Old Kingdom
painted limestone pair-statue of Kaitep and Hetepheres.*

*So when I started thinking of what I wanted to create for this
exhibition I felt I wanted to explore how the collection affected me
on several levels; first on a spiritual one, the effect of living in a
polytheistic society with many important female deities; then on
the personal level, examining the family likeness and the different
ways to interpret an ancient or personal history and how they are
read in the context of the museum.* rk 1994

6
Kaitep and Hetepheres painted limestone (about 2300 BC,
probably from Giza, BM EA 1181, height 47.5 cm)

6

7 8

9

7
Rita Keegan sketching an Ancient Egyptian comb

8
Untitled Rita Keegan, 1994, artefacts used in installation,
late 19th–early 20th century

9
Untitled Rita Keegan, 1994, still from CD ROM installation

kate whiteford

18 : 19   Kate Whiteford was born in Glasgow and lives in London.

---

*The Ptahshepses door has for me an extraordinary presence.
This is due partly to its architectural quality and also to its
incised hieroglyphs, which still retain traces of earth-red and
green pigment. The ancient Egyptian false door is a fascinating
concept, since it represents the transition point between one state
of being and another.*

*I felt an immediate rapport with this door and began to
consider parallels in my own work. I often use red and green in
my paintings at maximum hue, as they burn themselves into the
retina, creating an after-image in the mind. This could be read as
a metaphor for memory. By playing with our perceptive faculties
the painting hovers somewhere between reality and non-reality
and this duality seems to tie in with ancient Egyptian ideas.*

*To emphasise the connections with the false door of
Ptahshepses I chose to build the painting in multiple panels to
create an architectural form.*   kw 1994

10
False Door of Ptahshepses (about 2450 BC, from Saqqara,
BM EA 682, limestone, height 3.66 m). The so-called false door
was the most important part of an Egyptian tomb-chapel. Made of
stone, it functioned as a kind of magic doorway, through which, it
was believed, the spirit of the deceased person could pass and
receive nourishment in the afterlife

10

11

12

13

14

igor mitoraj

Igor Mitoraj, born 1942, in Oederan, Germany, of Polish parents,
is currently living in Pietrasanta, Italy.

Although ravaged by time, monuments of vanished civilisations
may take on an alternative aesthetic beauty in contemporary eyes
and Mitoraj often recreates the effects of time on the surfaces of
antiquities. By the same token Mitoraj's works are not fragments
but complete in their own right.

While making my sculpture for this exhibition I felt lost like
a grain of sand in the desert of Egypt. What do the immense eyes
of the statues see, looking inside their soul and gazing for
centuries at their shadows in the light of the sun and the moon?
How is it possible to describe the magnetic force that this ancient
civilisation releases? I have tried to convey a fraction of what
seems to be a mystical communion between Egypt, Greece and the
Far East - an extremely difficult task and practically impossible.
Art is the real time machine, that allows us to approach so far
a shore.   im 1994

15
Thsuki-No-Hikari ('Moonlight') Igor Mitoraj, 1991, bronze,
3.14 × 3.49 × 2.45 m. Produced in the Del Chiaro Foundry,
Pietrasanta

16
Fragment of a Colossal Head found near the ruins of Heliopolis,
Egypt. From *Description de L'Égypte, Antiquités* (Paris 1823),
Vol. V, pl. 27

time machine

17

17
Eclisse ('Eclipse') Igor Mitoraj, 1994, white marble head, 35 cm × 29 cm, in grano-diorite libation bowl of Mentuemhat (about 660 BC, from Thebes, BM EA 1292). The bowl is decorated with the head of the goddess Hathor

18
Iron Shadows (detail) Igor Mitoraj, 1994, cast iron, height (complete) 2.1 m. Produced in the Mariani Foundry, Pietrasanta

opposite 18

marc quinn

Marc Quinn, born in London, 1964, currently lives in London.

The location of the frog in the sculpture coincides with that of the dormant 'primitive' part of the human brain. In ancient Egypt the frog was regarded as a powerful protective deity closely associated with birth.

The frog used in this installation is a North American Wood Frog (*Rana sylvatica*). The Wood Frog freezes solid during the winter and thaws in the spring. It is one of a variety of cold-blooded animals with natural ability to survive freezing during their winter hibernation.

This exhibit was conceived with the assistance of Professor Jack R Layne, Department of Biology, Slippery Rock University, Pennsylvania, and installed following consultation with London Zoo. The refrigeration unit was specially designed by Bar Refrigeration.

The British Museum collections prove to me that however society or technology may evolve, human thought, emotions and aspirations remain little changed over time.

I see this sculpture as an evolutionary bungee jump.   mq 1994

19
Frog sculpture of andesite porphyry (about 3100 BC, BM EA 66837, height 12.3 cm). The frog goddess, Heket, was associated with conception and birth/rebirth

20
Working drawing Mark Quinn, 1994

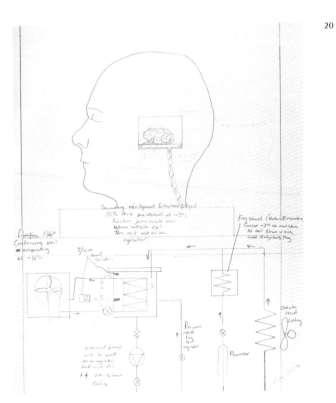

time machine

21

22

21
The Wood Frog (*Rana sylvatica*)

22
Predynastic mummy (about 3500 BC, from Gebelein,
BM EA 32752, length 1.51 m). The body has been preserved
naturally by the hot dry sand in which it was buried. In the
predynastic period the body was always placed in a foetal position
and sometimes covered with a skin or matting, as if asleep

23
Frog (computer simulation) Marc Quinn, 1994, mixed media

opposite 23

jiří kolář

Jiří Kolář, born 1914 in Protivin, Czechoslovakia, currently lives in Paris.

Using innumerable collage techniques, he makes frequent references to the history of art in his work, which is charged with poetry and wit, challenging normal perception. This is evident in both the two-dimensional works and the collage-covered cat made for this exhibition.

It was probably the cat's protective qualities against vermin that first brought it widespread respect and a prominent place in the personal religion of ordinary people in ancient Egypt. Later, the cat became associated with the Sun God, Ra, and attained special significance as the animal sacred to the daughter of Ra, Bastet. Hundreds of figures of cats were dedicated as votive offerings in her temple at Bubastis, in order that the donor might share in the goddess's grace.

The Gayer-Anderson cat is perhaps the most spectacular example of such temple gifts. The scarab-beetles on the head and chest symbolise the cat's connection with the rising sun. The wadjet-eye pendant is also a solar symbol.

Kolář's major work for the exhibition envelops a replica of this famous cat.

24
Self Portrait Jiří Kolář, 1980, Crumplage, 26.7cm × 62.3 cm

25
Untitled Jiří Kolář, 1993, torn postcard of Rosetta Stone, 10.5cm × 15 cm

26
Limestone pair-statue of Khaemwese and Nebettawy
(about 1275 BC, BM EA 51101, height 29 cm)

24

25

26

27 28 29 30
Untitled Jiří Kolář, 1994, four views of
pair-statue (see no. 26), one-cut collages,
25 × 32.5 cm

31
Untitled Jiří Kolář, 1994, collage-covered
resin replica of the Gayer-Anderson cat
(original of bronze, about 600 BC,
BM EA 64391, height 38 cm)

stephen cox

Stephen Cox was born in Bristol in 1946 and currently lives in London. He works primarily in stone that he often quarries in Egypt, having a special interest in imperial porphyry. In his statement he speaks of the god Min, the god of fertility. Min was particularly associated with the Eastern Desert, where he was venerated by workers quarrying stone such as breccia, diorite and porphyry.

One is closer to the Garden of Eden here in this desert where the Great God Min dwelt among these magic rocks, feted with lettuce – bestowing with his wand fecundity on those whose crunchy offerings were laid at his table. sc 1994

32
Graffito from the Wadi Hammamat Eastern Desert, Egypt, showing a king offering before the god Min (about 1650 BC)

33
Grano-diorite statue of a king (left) and the god Amun-Ra who is shown in the guise of the ithyphallic god Min (about 1350 BC, BM EA 21, height 1.68 m)

34
Porphyry bowl (about 2850 BC, BM EA 22823, height 10 cm)

32

33

34

35
Stephen Cox on 'Porphyry Mountain' in the
Eastern Desert of Egypt

36
Stone Bowls Stephen Cox, 1993. From left to
right: diorite, height 8.5 cm; pegmatite, height
7.8 cm; imperial porphyry, height 7.5 cm

37
Flask Stephen Cox, 1991, sculpture made from
Hammamat Breccia, height 1.83 m

35

36

time machine

martin riches

Martin Riches was born on the Isle of Wight in 1942 and has been living in Berlin since 1969. Since 1978 he has built a series of machines which perform fundamental human activities: Walking Machines, Drawing Machines, Writing Machines and Music Machines.

This small sound-sculpture attempts to pronounce the name of the Ancient Egyptian Sun God: RA. Visitors are invited to depress the bellows gently. It is not necessary to press very hard; the interior of the shrine, hewn out of solid granite, is an almost perfect reflector of sound and is beautifully resonant.

During the past few years I have become particularly interested in the problem of speech synthesis – but using acoustic rather than electronic methods. The main result so far has been my 'Talking Machine', a mechanical speech synthesiser which speaks with specially designed 'organ pipes', each of them being in fact a model of the human mouth. The Talking Machine has 32 of these pipes, all different and each corresponding to a different speech-sound. The valves which control the air supply to these pipes are operated by a computer. In English it is capable of speaking a few hundred words and forming sentences and it can also count in Japanese and German.

It was James Putnam, the initiator of this exhibition, who made the startling suggestion that my exhibit should be housed inside this shrine. To avoid disturbing the shrine with bunches of computer cables running in and out of it, I decided that the sound should be produced and controlled manually – by operating a bellows. Having no computer, and depending entirely on the skill or luck of the operator, my 'RA machine' will speak its name a little differently each time – and I am happy that this should be so.

'Rrr' plus 'Ah' equals 'Ra'. The initial 'Rrr' sound is produced by a wooden component which simulates the movement of the tongue inside the mouth. The curved wooden vessel, inside which it moves, is a hollow resonator that roughly reproduces the shape we make inside our mouths when we make the sound 'Ah'; it is based on an X-ray photograph of someone speaking that sound. The square red box underneath this 'mouth' contains a reed which reproduces the sound of the vocal chords. The bellows are the lungs. In other words, the complete instrument is a working model of the human vocal tract. The exhibit is constructed almost entirely of various kinds of plywood, a material first used by the Ancient Egyptians. An Ancient Egyptian craftsman would have had no difficulty in constructing this entire exhibit and there are no lack of precedents, since there are numerous legends and descriptions of talking statues and automata from Egypt.

As soon as I had managed to get the 'RA' mechanism to speak, I noticed that the round metal disc, which I just happened to be using as a counterweight on the 'tongue' component, strongly suggested the sun. It followed that its rising and falling motion could be interpreted as representing the passage of the sun across the sky. Having inadvertently introduced the symbolism, I decided to continue in this vein and added the doors to the upper part of the plinth. These can be seen as a reference to a mechanism devised by Hero of Alexandria, which opened and closed the doors of a shrine when a fire was lit on the altar.

May RA regard my activities with forebearance.

mr 1994

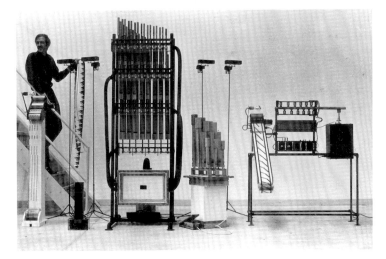

38
The so-called
'Colossi of Memnon'
(statues of King
Amenophis III, Thebes,
about 1400 BC,
quartzite, height 21 m),
one of them a
legendary 'singing
statue'

39
Martin Riches and some
of his machines

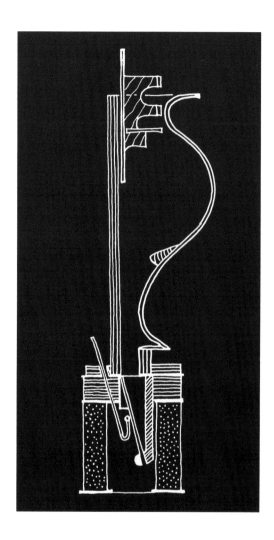

40

41

42

40
The RA voice pipe Martin Riches, 1994.
From top to bottom: the 'Rrr' mechanism, the
mouth resonator, the reed (blue-print drawing)

41
RA Martin Riches, 1994, height 71 cm

42
RA in a granite monolithic shrine
(143–137 BC, from Philae, BM EA 1134,
height 2.5 m). This shrine was originally sited in
the most sacred part of a temple. A cult statue
of a deity would have been placed inside

peter randall-page

Peter Randall-Page was born in Essex, England, in 1954
and currently lives in Devon.

*For me, Egyptian sculpture at its best is unsurpassed and
the Egyptian Sculpture Gallery in the British Museum contains
pieces which have been of great importance in the development
of my own sculpture. It is above all its ability to convey a sense
of internal dynamics which makes Egyptian carving so
powerful. It is the relationship between surface and volume,
the tension between skin and flesh, which can draw the
imagination inwards and towards the centre. This has become
a major preoccupation in my own sculpture and is epitomised
by many of the works in this gallery.*

*My piece is based on the Ouroboros, the emblematic
serpent of Ancient Egypt and Greece that bites its own tail and
returns onto itself. The image is found quite independently in
many diverse cultures throughout the world and is generally
used to express the concept of infinity.*

*In Egyptian mythology the image of a snake is strongly
associated with the concept of time. The Ouroborus can be a
metaphor for spatial as well as temporal infinity – the created
world bordering everywhere on the uncreated , in the same way
as the future continually borders on the past.*

*In recent years I have made a number of pieces based on an
endless coil or loop folded and knotted into densely packed
compositions, and the paradoxical image of the Ouroboros is a
development of this idea. The twelve meandering loops
continue endlessly, yet disappear inside themselves. The coils
thicken into a membrane and a lip where an infinite process
begins and ends.*

*Needless to say, it is a great honour to be able to exhibit this
new work in such noble and ancient company.*

*This sculpture will eventually form part of a
permanent installation in Kilkenny, Republic of Ireland.
When finally installed, a tree will be planted in the
central space.* pr-p 1994

43
Papyrus of Herweben, vignette
(about 950 BC, Cairo Museum). The
Sun God as child, encircled by the never
ending Ouroboros, carried by the celestial
cow and the lions of the horizon

44
Peter Randall-Page with his work in
progress

45
Drawing for 'Ouroborus' Peter Randall-Page, 1994, charcoal on paper, 58 × 76 cm

46
Peter Randall-Page at an early stage of the work

47
Ouroboros Peter Randall-Page, 1994, 76.5 × 191 × 187 cm, one of two elements
in Kilkenny limestone of the sculpture *Forbidden Fruit*, to be completed 1995

time machine

andy goldsworthy

Andy Goldsworthy was born in 1956 in Cheshire, England, and is
currently living in Dumfries, Scotland.

It is difficult to deal with a room containing
fragments from such a rich culture. If I were to make
something self-consciously Egyptian there would be a
danger of it being superficial. I also wanted to avoid
using the room as a library and making too literal an
interpretation. I have also felt this response when
working in a country with a strong cultural tradition. In
the Arctic, Australia and Japan I responded first to the
land, the place. It is not that I am avoiding a cultural
exchange, but feel this should come through the making.

My first response to the Egyptian Sculpture Gallery
was of sand. Sand is somewhere between stone and earth.
It can be compressed hard and yet it can become fluid. It
has a sense of strength, fragility and movement. The
work would flow through the room – touching the
sculptures and incorporating them into its form to give a
feeling of the underlying geological and cultural energies
that flow through the sculptures. I want to think of the
landscape and the life from where they came.

The project was initially turned down because it
would have restricted access to the room. James Putnam
contacted me later and suggested that we make the work
for a day, photograph it, then remove it, to be represented
in the exhibition as a memory. I found this a fascinating
idea and one that would make the work stronger. That
something was there, but has gone, touches on the
relationship between an object and its origin. To think
beyond the object to what we cannot see.

I have also made works for the sarcophagi. I initially
responded to them as stone containers offering protection
to objects inside. A work made with leaves is a
celebration of growth, yet cannot work without
expressing some anticipation of death, in a way that
understands that death is a part of growth.

In some ways I wanted to use familiar forms, works
that have appeared already, so that the place will draw
out new meanings. It is interesting that all the forms are
the most stylised that I work with. In different places I
have felt uncomfortable about using these forms, because
they have the feeling of design. Yet the Egyptian Sculpture
Gallery, with its strong element of stylisation and
design,will I think make them work differently. It makes
them more appropriate. The sarcophagi are not just
containers of death, they are containers of life, in that out
of death comes life.   ag 1994

[Significantly, the ancient Egyptian term for 'sarcophagus' was
'neb ankh' meaning 'lord of life'.]

48
Stonework Andy Goldsworthy, 1994, in the schist
sarcophagus of the God's Adorer, Ankhnesneferibre
(about 530 BC, from Thebes, BM EA 32, length 2.6 m).
On the floor is a carving of the Goddess of the West

49
Sandwork Andy Goldsworthy, 1994, in the green
breccia sarcophagus of King Nectanebo II (about 345
BC, from Alexandria, BM EA 10, length 3.13 m)

48

49

andy goldsworthy

50
Leafwork
Andy Goldsworthy, 1994, sweet chestnut leaves, in chestnut wooden box within grano-diorite sarcophagus of Hapmen (about 600 BC, BM EA 23, length 2.75 m)

51
Leafwork
Andy Goldsworthy, 1994, sweet chestnut leaves, in a black basalt libation bowl (about 625 BC, BM EA 1386, diameter 78 cm)

52
Sandwork
Andy Goldsworthy, 1994, made from thirty tons of sand, in Egyptian Sculpture Gallery, The British Museum (temporary installation, October 22–25, 1994)

50

51

alexander mihaylovich

Alexander Mihaylovich was born in 1958 in New York.
He is currently living in Los Angeles, California.

---

*The 'Colossus of Menes' celebrates the founder of
Dynastic Egypt, reflecting the Egyptian style of monumental
expression in its immense proportions. I chose to represent Menes,
since he is the legendary King whom the Ancient Egyptians
themselves venerated as the great unifier of Upper and Lower
Egypt. As no contemporary images of him have survived, my
work is a composite of numerous portraits of Egyptian Pharaohs.
A king that lived some 5000 years ago, Menes is the
personification of the unifying principle in all of us.*

*The scale of the surrounding sculptures and architectural
fragments in the gallery inspired me to create an installation of
such a size. I had to plan it with great care in order to make it a
safe, stable and free-standing structure. The difficult task of its
construction took all of seven months. The specially weighted base
is designed to anchor it down and the various box sections are
engineered employing a bridge-like system of trusses. The sections
have been veneered with galvanised metal patinated by hand.
The most detailed and time-consuming veneers were the
limestone-like slabs into which I carved the hieroglyphs. This text
is adapted from a scene in the temple at Abydos which depicts
King Seti I and his son making offerings to the cartouches of his
ancestors featuring the name of Menes in the first cartouche.*

*I would like my work to stand in humble tribute to a
great ancient civilisation. I can only hope that 5000 years from
now our modern achievements are remembered with such
reverence.*   am 1994

53
Alexander Mihaylovich with maquette
for **Colossus of Menes**, 1993

54
**The king-list in the Temple of Seti I
at Abydos** (about 1300 BC), with detail of
Menes cartouche

alexander mihaylovich

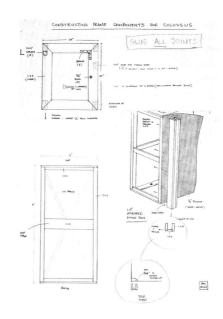

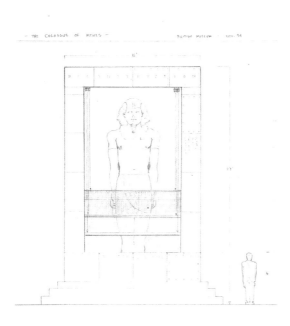

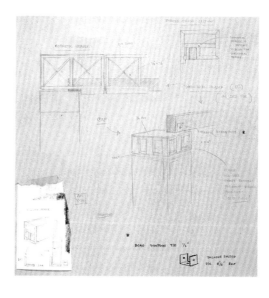

55 56 57
Colossus of Menes Preliminary drawings,
Alexander Mihaylovich, 1993

58
Colossus of Menes Alexander Mihaylovich, 1994,
mixed media, 4.88 × 7.62 m

liliane karnouk

Liliane Karnouk was born in Cairo, Egypt, in 1944. She now
resides in both Canada and Cairo.

Her installation involves the use of live date-palms, grown with
the aid of Dr Sinclair Mantell of the University of London, using a
technique known as micro-propagation. This technique allows
easily grown species in short supply to be produced very rapidly.
The cast-iron railings were manufactured by Anthony Thomson
Smith Railings.

---

*There is a Bara legend from Madagascar which tells the story
of how death came about. The first man and first woman were
asked at the beginning of time to choose between two deaths.
The first was to die like the moon and be reborn over and over
again. The second was to die like a tree and regenerate through
seeds.*

*According to the legend most men and women chose the latter,
so did the Egyptians… but not quite. The ancient Egyptians
defied death by becoming Osiris. They died like trees and became
immortal like the moon.*

*My work over the years has always paid homage to that
defiance. My choice of materials has constantly been in tune with
the Egyptian tradition of assuming and integrating polarities: the
spear and the test tube; cast-iron fences and the growing cells of a
palm tree.* lk 1994

59
Scene painted on a wooden funerary box
showing its deceased owner receiving water
from a tree-goddess (about 1290 BC,
BM EA 41549, height 34.5 cm)

60
The god of the dead, Osiris, with corn growing
from his body, receives libation
(first century BC–first century AD, wall-relief,
Temple of Philae)

59

60

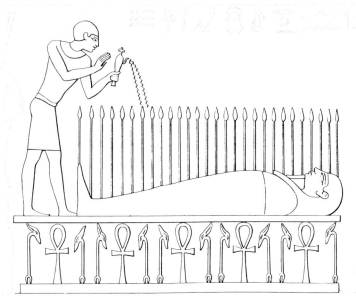

61

62

61
Test-tube containing live date-palm

62
Detail of installation showing railings, test-tubes
with palms, and side of the sarcophagus
decorated with frieze of gods. Liliane Karnouk,
1994

63
Liliane Karnouk, 1994, installation surrounding
granite sarcophagus of Nesisut (about 450 BC,
from Giza, BM EA 30, length 2.47 m)

time machine

The British Museum should not be looked on as a collection of dead art disconnected from our own times.

It gives me a chance, gratefully to admit my debt to the B.M., + all I have learned there about world sculpture

henry moore

acknowledgements

For their invaluable help during the preparation of
time machine, I am especially grateful to Andrew Geraghty
and Georgina Evans, who have acted as curatorial assistants,
and to Janet Peckham, who has taken so many excellent
photographs.

I would also like to thank the following for their help
and encouragement with the **time machine** exhibition :
Lambert Monet and Henk Rijkers (Rijkers Art Diffusion),
Clive Adams, Michael Hue-Williams, Jay Jopling,
Richard Dyer (Third Text), John Carpenter (Chart Design),
Peter McGrath (Groundwork), Raymond Gresham (Studio
Tone), Martin Holmes (Quest International), Geoffrey
Pflaumer (Pioneer GB), Frank Boyd and Gary Stuart (Artec),
Claire Lilley (Yorkshire Sculpture Park), Kevin Richardson
(Momart), Marjorie Althorpe-Guyton (Arts Council of
England), Mariam Sharpe (London Arts Board), Allen Jones,
Norman Rosenthal, Roman Kames, Kiki Smith, Dr Sinclair
Mantell, John Meakin (ILACON), Tony Smith, Dr Terry
Friedman, Nigel Tufnel, Nicholas Reeves, Anthony Fawcett,
Emma Stowe (The Henry Moore Foundation), Yukiko
Kakuta, Renée Friedman, Roxie Walker, Edward Giddens
(Paramount Studios), Pat Terry, Jenny May, Stephen Quirke,
John Hayman, John Reeve, George Hart, Calum Storrie,
Julian Calder, Ellie Hall and all the volunteers who helped
with the Andy Goldsworthy Sandwork

James Putnam
British Museum

time machine : *Ancient Egypt and Contemporary Art*
an exhibition at The British Museum
1st December 1994 – 26th February 1995

© 1994
The artists, and The Trustees of the British Museum
London WC1B 3DG

ISBN 0 86159 997 7

Edited by James Putnam and W Vivian Davies

Unless stated below, photography courtesy of the
artists and the British Museum Photographic Service
Julian Calder   foldout, nos. 48, 49, 50, 52
Chris Chapman   nos. 44, 46, 47
Enrico Chelli   no. 18
Jerry Hardman-Jones   no. 15
Joel D Levinson   no. 58
Henry Moore Foundation   p59

Logo design
Sean Gaherty

Publication design/production
Groundwork, Skipton

Reprographics
Leeds Photo Litho

Printing and binding
Jackson Wilson, Leeds; Smith Settle, Otley